Introduction

Learn to make a beautiful bargello quilt with ease. Bargello quilts can be fun and interesting to make. The techniques used are a bit different than block piecing and can be tweaked if you have a creative spirit. Strip piecing makes construction fast and easy, and allows you to keep track of color position.

There are many ways to assemble a bargello quilt. This book explores a few traditional ways and then goes beyond. If you're a quilter looking for fun, fast and easy techniques, this book has it all.

Bargello Quilts & Beyond bends the rules and explores the possibilities. This book has everything from very basic bargello assembly to outside-the-box creativity.

With the help of talented designers, we've put together a collection of fantastic patterns with variety and style—ones you'll thoroughly enjoy stitching. If you've been waiting for the right bargello book, it's here.

Table of Contents

Light-Headed Bargello

This easy bargello uses alternating strip sets
in similar color selections—one light and
one dark—to create the illusion of movement.

Designed & Quilted by Holly Daniels

Skill Level
Confident Beginner

Finished Size
Quilt Size: 53" x 63"

Materials
- 1 D strip each 3" x 40" of 10 blue tonals from dark to very light
- ⅜ yard white solid
- 2⅛ yards navy blue tonal
- 2⅝ yards medium blue tonal
- Backing to size
- Batting to size
- Thread
- Basic sewing tools and supplies

Project Notes
Read all instructions before beginning this project.

Stitch right sides together using a ¼" seam allowance unless otherwise specified.

Refer to a favorite quilting guide for specific techniques.

Materials and cutting lists assume 40" of usable fabric width.

Cutting

From white solid:
- Cut 3 (3" by fabric width) C strips.

From navy blue tonal:
- Cut 21 (3" by fabric width) A strips.

From medium blue tonal:
- Cut 17 (3" by fabric width) B strips.
- Cut 6 (2" by fabric width) E/F strips.
- Cut 7 (2¼") by fabric width binding strips.

Completing the Strip Sets

1. Sew an A strip to a B strip along length to make an A-B strip set; press seams toward A. Repeat to make a total of 13 A-B strip sets.

2. Join the A-B strip sets to make an A-B section as shown in Figure 1.

Figure 1

3. Join the A end of the A-B section with the B end to make a tube as shown in Figure 2; press seam toward A.

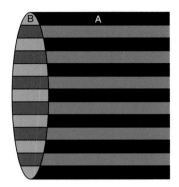

Figure 2

4. Lay the tube on a cutting mat, aligning seams; trim one end to make a straight edge.

5. Cut the tube into 13 (2½") loops as shown in Figure 3.

Figure 3

6. Divide the loops into one pile of seven loops for W and one pile of six loops for X.

7. Use a seam ripper to remove one B segment from the loops in the W pile leaving an A segment at each end of the strips. Trim both end A segments to 1½" as shown in Figure 4.

Figure 4   **Figure 5**

8. Repeat step 7, removing one A segment from the loops in the X pile and trimming B to 1½" as shown in Figure 5.

9. Set aside the W and X strips.

10. Arrange and join the remaining A and B strips with the C and D strips to make a strip set as shown in Figure 6, placing D strips in order from dark to very light as shown; press seams toward darker fabrics.

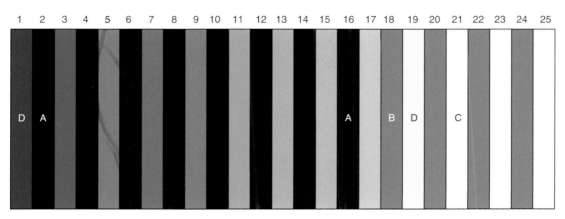

Figure 6

11. Join strip 1 and strip 25 to make a tube as in step 3.

12. Repeat step 4.

13. Cut the tube into 12 (2½") loops.

14. Divide the loops into two piles of six loops each. Label one pile Y and the other pile Z.

15. Use a seam ripper to remove the darkest blue D segment from each loop in the Y pile to make Y strips, leaving a white C segment at the top of the strip and a navy blue A segment at the bottom as shown in Figure 7.

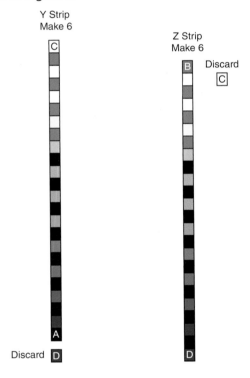

Figure 7   Figure 8

16. Repeat step 15, removing the end white C segment from each loop in the Z pile to make Z strips, leaving the darkest blue D segment on the bottom and a medium blue B segment at the top as shown in Figure 8.

17. Arrange and join the W, X, Y and Z strips in sets of two, then in sets of four and so on until you have stitched all strips together to create the bargello center referring to Figure 9 for placement of strips; press seams open.

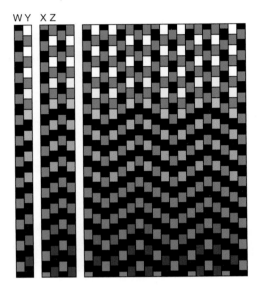

Figure 9

Completing the Quilt Top
1. Join the E/F strips on the short ends to make a long strip; press. Subcut strip into two each 2" x 60½" E strips and 2" x 53½" F strips.

2. Sew the E strips to opposite long sides and F strips to the top and bottom of the bargello center to complete the quilt top; press.

Completing the Quilt
1. Sandwich the batting between the pieced top and a prepared backing piece; baste layers together. Quilt as desired.

2. When quilting is complete, remove basting and trim batting and backing fabric even with raw edges of the pieced top.

3. Prepare binding and stitch to quilt front edges, matching raw edges, mitering corners and overlapping ends. Fold binding to back side and stitch in place. ●

Tube Construction

Many bargello designs are made using tube construction. The tube is made with variety of strips joined on the long edges to make a large strip set. After pressing, the end strips in the strip set are joined to make a tube. The tube is then cut into tube segments called loops. The segments can be all the same width or varying widths, depending on the design. The design is formed by removing stitches between two segments in each loop to make flat strips. In some designs, segments are removed from one or both ends, again depending on the design.

The tube construction method is easy and eliminates cutting and sewing individual pieces. It's easy to play with the strips to create different bargello designs.

Light-Headed Bargello
Assembly Diagram 53" x 63"

And the Beat Goes On

Strip sets of alternating solid strips and matched seams create the beat.

Designed & Quilted by Holly Daniels

Skill Level
Confident Beginner

Finished Size
Quilt Size: 45" x 15"

Materials
- 1 D strip each 1½" x 40" purple, gold, pink, blue and yellow solids
- 1 yard green solid
- 1⅛ yards white solid
- Backing to size
- Batting to size
- Thread
- Basic sewing tools and supplies

Project Notes
Read all instructions before beginning this project.

Stitch right sides together using a ¼" seam allowance unless otherwise specified.

Refer to a favorite quilting guide for specific techniques.

Materials and cutting lists assume 40" of usable fabric width.

Cutting

From green solid:
- Cut 10 (1½" by fabric width) C strips.
- Cut 4 (2¼") by fabric width binding strips.

From white solid:
- Cut 1 (8½" by fabric width) A strip.
- Cut 4 (1½" by fabric width) B strips.
- Cut 1 (15½" by fabric width) strip.
  Subcut strip into 22 (1½" x 15½") E strips.

Completing the Runner Top
1. Arrange and join the A strip with the B, C and D strips along length to make a strip set referring to Figure 1 for color order; press seams toward the C strips.

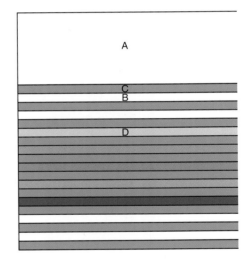

Figure 1

Here's a Tip
Change directions when stitching strips together in strip sets and when joining pieced strips with the E strips to reduce distortion.

2. Join the A end of the strip set with the C end to make a tube as shown in Figure 2; press seam toward the C strip.

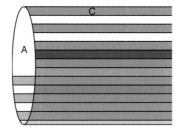

Figure 2

3. Lay the tube on a cutting mat, aligning seams. Trim one end to make a straight edge.

4. Subcut tube into 23 (1½") loops as shown in Figure 3.

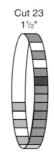

Cut 23
1½"

Figure 3

5. Use a seam ripper to remove the stitches between certain segments of each cut loop; remove and discard segments as indicated. For example, strip 1 is separated between the A segment and a C segment. It uses the entire A segment and just seven of the B/C/D segments. Remove stitches and discard the remaining segments below the seventh piece to make the 15½"-long strip 1 as shown in Figure 4.

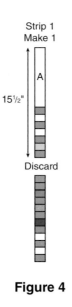

Strip 1
Make 1

15½"

A

Discard

Figure 4

6. Some strips do not use the entire width of the A segment. For strip 2, again separate the loop between the A segment and a C segment. Count nine segments below the A segment, remove stitches and discard remaining segments at the bottom. Measure and trim strip to 15½", trimming excess from the A end as shown in Figure 5.

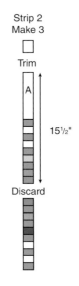

Strip 2
Make 3

Trim

A

15½"

Discard

Figure 5

7. Continue this process to create 1½" x 15½" strips 3–10 referring to Figure 6 to make each strip and the number needed of each. Note that the loops are not always separated at the same seam and that A is not always part of the completed strip.

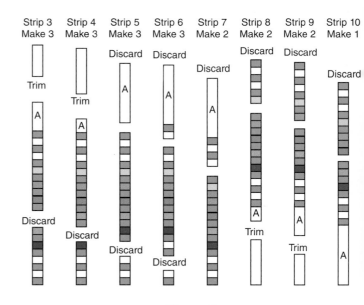

Figure 6

8. Arrange and join the strips in groups with E strips as shown in Figure 7; press seams toward E.

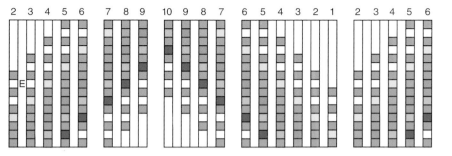

Figure 7

9. Join the groups with E strips as shown in Figure 8 to complete the runner top; press seams toward E.

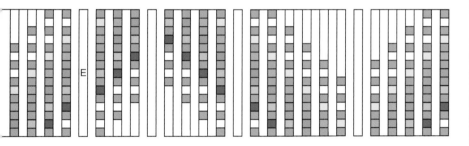

Figure 8

Completing the Runner

1. Sandwich the batting between the pieced top and a prepared backing piece; baste layers together. Quilt as desired.

2. When quilting is complete, remove basting and trim batting and backing fabric even with raw edges of the pieced top.

3. Prepare binding and stitch to runner front edges, matching raw edges, mitering corners and overlapping ends. Fold binding to back side and stitch in place. ●

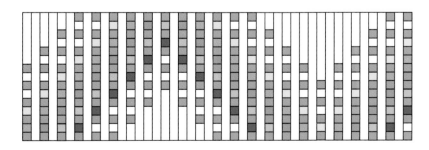

And the Beat Goes On
Placement Diagram 45" x 15"

Robin's Egg Blue

This beauty goes together much more easily than you'd think.
Piece the bargello blocks, add the sashing and you're done.

Design by Gina Gempesaw
Quilted by Carole Whaling

Skill Level
Intermediate

Finished Size
Quilt Size: 66" x 66"
Block Size: 12" x 12" finished
Number of Blocks: 16

Materials
- ⅔ yard light blue print
- ⅔ yard cream tonal
- 1⅛ yards tan tonal
- 1¼ yards dark brown tonal
- 1½ yards dark blue tonal
- 2 yards turquoise tonal
- Backing to size
- Batting to size
- Thread
- Basic sewing tools and supplies

Project Notes
Read all instructions before beginning this project.

Stitch right sides together using a ¼" seam allowance unless otherwise specified.

Refer to a favorite quilting guide for specific techniques.

Materials and cutting lists assume 40" of usable fabric width.

Cutting
When cutting half strips (20"), if fabric is wider than 40", cut the fabric width strip in half to make two equal-length strips.

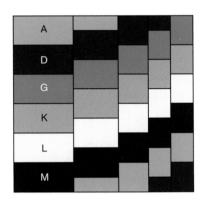

Z Block
12" x 12" Finished Block
Make 8

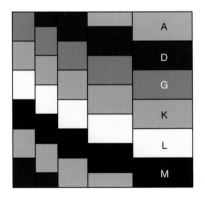

Reverse Z Block
12" x 12" Finished Block
Make 8

From light blue print:
- Cut 8 (2½" by fabric width) K strips.
  Subcut 1 strip into 2 (2½" x 20") K1 strips.

From cream tonal:
- Cut 8 (2½" by fabric width) L strips.
  Subcut 1 strip into 2 (2½" x 20") L1 strips.

From tan tonal:

- Cut 6 (2½" by fabric width) A strips.
  Subcut 1 strip into 2 (2½" x 20") A1 strips.
- Cut 4 (1½" by fabric width) B strips.
- Cut 1 (8½" by fabric width) strip.
  Subcut strip into 2 (8½" x 20") C strips.

From dark brown tonal:

- Cut 8 (2½" by fabric width) D strips.
  Subcut 2 strips into 4 (2½" x 20") D1 strips.
- Cut 2 (1½" by fabric width) E strips.
- Cut 6 (2" by fabric width) F strips.

From dark blue tonal:

- Cut 8 (2½" by fabric width) M strips.
  Subcut 1 strip into 1 (2½" x 20") M1 strip.
- Cut 3 (1½" by fabric width) strips.
  Subcut strips into 6 (1½" x 20") N strips.
- Cut 7 (2¼" by fabric width) binding strips.

From turquoise tonal:

- Cut 9 (2½" by fabric width) G strips.
  Subcut 2 strips into 1 (2½" x 20") G1 strip
  and 9 (2½") I squares.
- Cut 1 (1½" by fabric width) strip.
  Subcut strip into 2 (1½" x 20") H strips.
- Cut 7 (5" by fabric width) J strips.

Completing the Strips

1. Join one each A, D, G, K, L and M strip along length in the order listed to make a Q strip set; press. Repeat to make a second Q strip set.

Here's a Tip

Press seams carefully to avoid distortion when joining strips to make strip sets. Square the edges of the strip sets after cutting four to six segments to guarantee straight and perfectly square strips.

2. Subcut the Q strip sets into 16 (4½" x 12½") Q strips as shown in Figure 1.

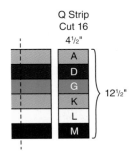

Figure 1

3. Repeat step 1 with B, D, G, K, L, M and B strips to make two R strip sets. Subcut the R strip sets into 16 (3½" x 12½") R strips as shown in Figure 2.

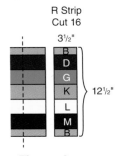

Figure 2

4. Repeat step 1 with D, G, K, L, M and A strips to make one S strip set. Subcut the S strip set into 16 (2½" x 12½") S strips as shown in Figure 3.

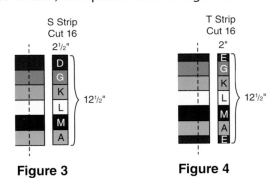

Figure 3   **Figure 4**

5. Repeat step 1 with E, G, K, L, M, A and E strips to make one T strip set. Subcut the T strip set into 16 (2" x 12½") T strips as shown in Figure 4.

6. Repeat step 1 with G, K, L, M, A and D strips to make one U strip set. Subcut the U strip set into 16 (2" x 12½") U strips as shown in Figure 5.

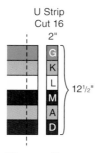

U Strip
Cut 16
2"

G
K
L
M
A
D

12½"

Figure 5

7. Repeat step 1 with N, C, D1 and N strips to make one V strip set. Subcut the V strip set into eight 2½" x 12½" V sashing strips as shown in Figure 6.

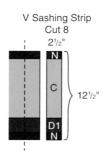

V Sashing Strip
Cut 8
2½"

N
C
D1
N

12½"

Figure 6

8. Repeat step 1 with N, C, D1 and H strips to make one W strip set. Subcut the W strip set into four 2½" x 12½" W sashing strips as shown in Figure 7.

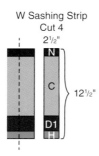

W Sashing Strip
Cut 4
2½"

N
C
D1
H

12½"

Figure 7

9. Repeat step 1 with N, A1, D1, G1, K1, L1 and N strips to make one X strip set. Subcut the X strip set into four 2½" x 12½" X sashing strips as shown in Figure 8.

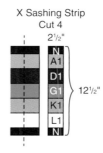

X Sashing Strip
Cut 4
2½"

N
A1
D1
G1
K1
L1
N

12½"

Figure 8

10. Repeat step 1 with H, K1, L1, M1, A1, D1 and N strips to make one Y strip set. Subcut the Y strip set into eight 2½" x 12½" Y sashing strips as shown in Figure 9.

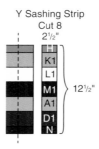

Y Sashing Strip
Cut 8
2½"

H
K1
L1
M1
A1
D1
N

12½"

Figure 9

Completing the Blocks

1. Select one each Q, R, S, T and U strip and join in the order given to complete one Z Block as shown in Figure 10; press. Repeat to make a total of eight Z Blocks.

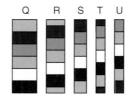

Q   R   S   T   U

Figure 10

2. Select one each U, T, S, R and Q strip and join in the order given to complete one Reverse Z Block as shown in Figure 11; press. Repeat to make a total of eight Reverse Z Blocks.

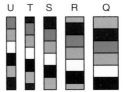

Figure 11

Completing the Quilt Top

1. Arrange and join the pieced blocks with the V, W, X and Y sashing strips and the I squares in block and sashing rows referring to Figure 12; press.

Figure 12

2. Join the block rows with the sashing rows to complete the pieced center; press.

3. Join the F strips on the short ends to make a long strip; press. Subcut strip into two each 2" x 54½" F1 and 2" x 57½" F2 strips. Sew the F1 strips to opposite sides and F2 strips to the top and bottom of the pieced center.

4. Join the J strips on the short ends to make a long strip; press. Subcut strip into two each 5" x 57½" J1 strips and 5" x 66½" J2 strips. Sew the J1 strips to opposite sides and J2 strips to the top and bottom of the pieced center to complete the quilt top; press.

Completing the Quilt

1. Sandwich the batting between the pieced top and a prepared backing piece; baste layers together. Quilt as desired.

2. When quilting is complete, remove basting and trim batting and backing fabric even with raw edges of the pieced top.

3. Prepare binding and stitch to quilt front edges, matching raw edges, mitering corners and overlapping ends. Fold binding to back side and stitch in place. ●

Inspiration

"Visiting the Southwest introduced me to beautiful turquoise and silver jewelry, which inspired this quilt." —Gina Gempesaw

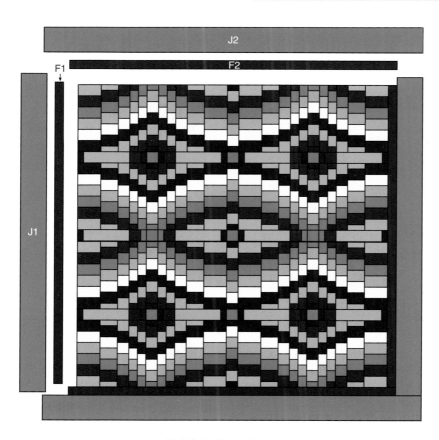

Robin's Egg Blue
Assembly Diagram 66" x 66"

Sunspots

Piece the bargello blocks, rotate them and add
sashing to create this unique setting.

Design by Gina Gempesaw
Quilted by Anne Cowan

Skill Level
Intermediate

Finished Size
Quilt Size: 66" x 66"
Block Size: 12" x 12" finished
Number of Blocks: 16

Materials
- ⅞ yard gold tonal
- ⅞ yard light blue tonal
- 1 yard orange print
- 1¼ yards light cream tonal
- 1⅜ yards black tonal
- 2⅛ yards gray print
- Backing to size
- Batting to size
- Thread
- Basic sewing tools and supplies

Project Notes
Read all instructions before beginning this project.

Stitch right sides together using a ¼" seam
allowance unless otherwise specified.

Refer to a favorite quilting guide for specific
techniques.

Materials and cutting lists assume 40" of usable
fabric width.

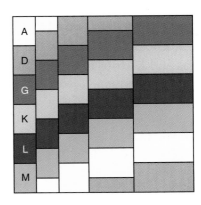

Sunspots
12" x 12" Finished Block
Make 16

Cutting

From gold tonal:
- Cut 9 (2½" by fabric width) K strips.

From light blue tonal:
- Cut 8 (2½" by fabric width) M strips.
- Cut 2 (1½" by fabric width) N strips.

From orange print:
- Cut 7 (2½" by fabric width) D strips.
- Cut 1 (2½" by fabric width) strips.
  Subcut strip into 5 (2½") E squares.
- Cut 4 (1½" by fabric width) F strips.

From light cream tonal:
- Cut 8 (2½" by fabric width) A strips.
- Cut 2 (1½" by fabric width) B strips.
- Cut 6 (2" by fabric width) C strips.

From black tonal:
- Cut 9 (2½" by fabric width) L strips.
- Cut 7 (2¼" by fabric width) binding strips.

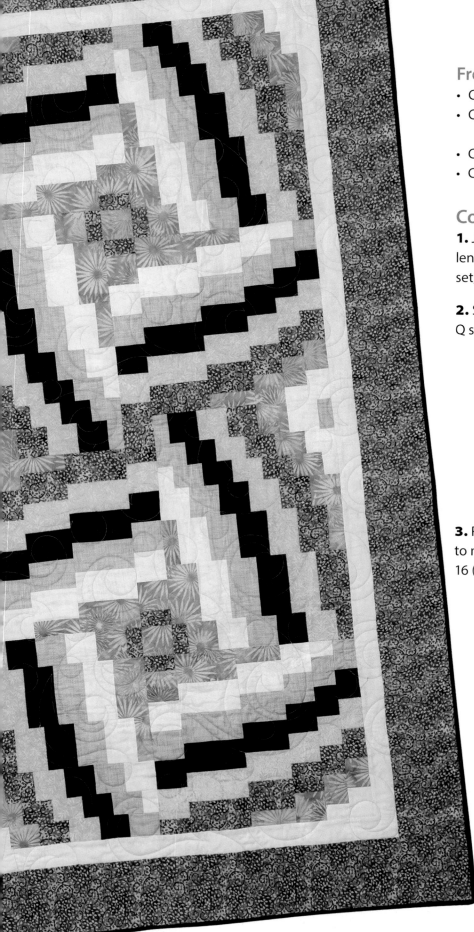

From gray print:

- Cut 8 (2½" by fabric width) G strips.
- Cut 1 (2½" by fabric width) strip.
  Subcut strip into 4 (2½") H squares.
- Cut 2 (1½" by fabric width) I strips.
- Cut 7 (5" by fabric width) J strips.

Completing the Strips

1. Join one each A, D, G, K, L and M strip along length in the order listed to make a Q strip set; press.

2. Subcut the Q strip set into 16 (2" x 12½") Q strips as shown in Figure 1.

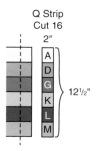

Figure 1

3. Repeat step 1 with B, D, G, K, L, M and B strips to make an R strip set. Subcut the R strip set into 16 (2" x 12½") R strips as shown in Figure 2.

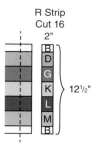

Figure 2

4. Repeat step 1 with D, G, K, L, M and A strips to make an S strip set. Subcut the S strip set into 16 (2½" x 12½") S strips as shown in Figure 3.

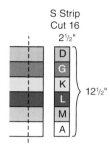

Figure 3

5. Repeat step 1 with F, G, K, L, M, A and F strips to make two T strip sets. Subcut the T strip sets into 16 (3½" x 12½") T strips as shown in Figure 4.

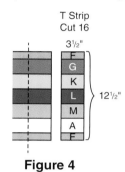

Figure 4

6. Repeat step 1 with G, K, L, M, A and D strips to make two U strip sets. Subcut the U strip sets into 16 (4½" x 12½") U strips as shown in Figure 5.

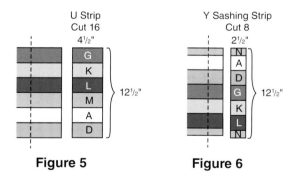

Figure 5   **Figure 6**

7. Repeat step 1 with N, A, D, G, K, L and N strips to make a Y strip set. Subcut the Y strip set into eight (2½" x 12½") Y sashing strips as shown in Figure 6.

8. Repeat step 1 with I, K, L, M, A, D and I strips to make a Z strip set. Subcut the Z strip set into 16 (2½" x 12½") Z sashing strips as shown in Figure 7.

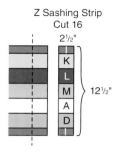

Figure 7

Completing the Blocks

1. Select one each Q, R, S, T and U strip and join in the order given to complete one Sunspots block as shown in Figure 8; press.

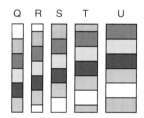

Figure 8

2. Repeat step 1 to make a total of 16 Sunspots blocks.

Completing the Quilt Top

1. Arrange and join the pieced blocks with the Y and Z sashing strips, and the E and H squares in block and sashing rows referring to Figure 9; press.

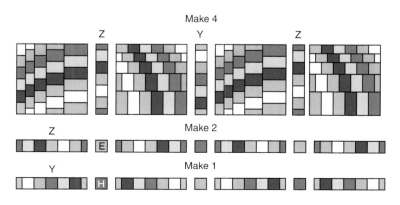

Figure 9

2. Join the block rows with the sashing rows in the order shown in Figure 10 to complete the pieced center; press.

3. Join the C strips on the short ends to make a long strip; press. Subcut strip into two each 2" x 54½" C1 and 2" x 57½" C2 strips. Sew the C1 strips to opposite sides and C2 strips to the top and bottom of the pieced center.

4. Join the J strips on the short ends to make a long strip; press. Subcut strip into two each 5" x 57½" J1 strips and 5" x 66½" J2 strips. Sew the J1 strips to opposite sides and J2 strips to the top and bottom of the pieced center to complete the quilt top; press.

Completing the Quilt

1. Sandwich the batting between the pieced top and a prepared backing piece; baste layers together. Quilt as desired.

2. When quilting is complete, remove basting and trim batting and backing fabric even with raw edges of the pieced top.

3. Prepare binding and stitch to quilt front edges, matching raw edges, mitering corners and overlapping ends. Fold binding to back side and stitch in place. ●

Inspiration

"Dark spots and flares on the sun's surface are quite fascinating and inspired the design and colors of this project." —Gina Gempesaw

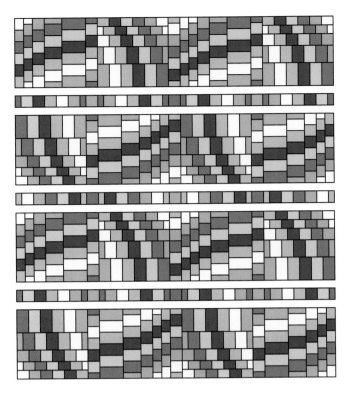

Figure 10

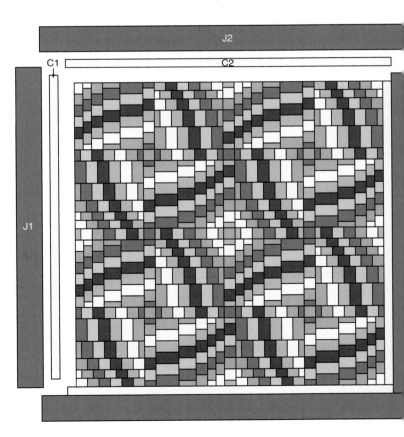

Sunspots
Assembly Diagram 66" x 66"

Olé

Here's your chance to make a bargello that's just the right size for a busy quilter. Add some fun appliqué for a personal look.

Designed & Quilted by Carol Streif

Skill Level
Intermediate

Finished Size
Quilt Size: 34½" x 38"

Materials
- ¼ yard each 8 bright solids
- ½ yard black solid
- ⅔ yard dark focus print
- ⅝ yard outer border fabric
- Backing to size
- Batting to size
- Thread
- ½ yard 18"-wide fusible web
- Basic sewing tools and supplies

Project Notes
Read all instructions before beginning this project.

Stitch right sides together using a ¼" seam allowance unless otherwise specified.

Refer to a favorite quilting guide for specific techniques.

Materials and cutting lists assume 42" of usable fabric width.

Here's a Tip

Fat quarters may be used instead of yardage. Cut four 2" by fabric width strips from each of the 10 fabrics used in the strip sets. The finished width of the strip sets must be at least 21"—wider is better.

Cutting
Prepare templates for flower shapes. Cut as directed and prepare for fusible appliqué referring to Raw-Edge Fusible Appliqué on page 29.

From each of the 8 bright solids:
- Cut 2 (2" by fabric width) strips (16 strips total).
    Cut each strip in half to make 4 (2" x 21") strips each fabric (32 half-strips total).

From black solid:
- Cut 2 (2" by fabric width) strips.
    Cut each strip in half to make 4 (2" x 21") strips.

From dark focus print:
- Cut 2 (2" by fabric width) strips.
    Cut each strip in half to make 4 (2" x 21") strips.
- Cut 4 (1" by fabric width) strips.
    Subcut strips into 2 (1" x 30½") A strips and 2 (1" x 28") B strips.
- Cut 4 (2¼" by fabric width) binding strips.

From outer border fabric:
- Cut 4 (4" by fabric width) strips.
    Trim strips to make 2 (4" x 31½") C strips and 2 (4" x 35") D strips.

Completing the Strip Sets
1. Select one 2" x 21" strip each of the eight bright solids, black solid and dark focus print—10 strips total.

2. Arrange these fabrics in the desired order and label each strip with its correct order number (1–10).

3. Join the fabric strips along length in numerical order, starting by sewing strip 1 to strip 2, strip 3 to strip 4, etc., and joining the pairs until the strip set is complete as shown in Figure 1. Do not press yet.

Make 4

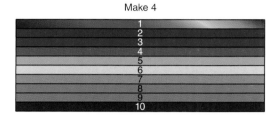

Figure 1

4. Repeat steps 1–3 to complete a total of four strip sets.

5. Join two strip sets to complete a larger strip set, joining strip 1 of one set to strip 10 of the other set as shown in Figure 2; press the seams of this larger set toward the top strip 1.

Make 2

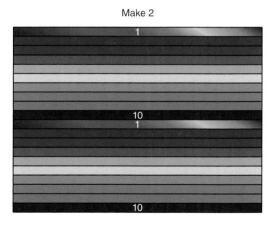

Figure 2

6. Repeat step 5 with the remaining two strip sets except press the seams toward the bottom strip 10.

7. Join the long edge of strip 1 with strip 10 to make tube 1 as shown in Figure 3; press seam in the same direction as the other seams in the tube. Repeat to make tube 2.

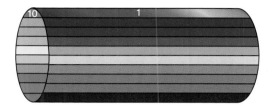

Figure 3

Completing the Bargello Center

1. Referring to Figure 4, cut eight 1", one 1½" and five 2" loops from tube 1 for the odd-numbered rows.

Odd-Numbered Rows

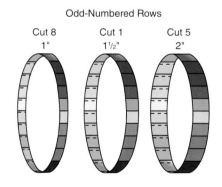

Cut 8 1" Cut 1 1½" Cut 5 2"

Figure 4

2. Referring to Figure 5, cut seven 1", three 1½", one 2" and three 2½" loops from tube 2 for the even-numbered rows.

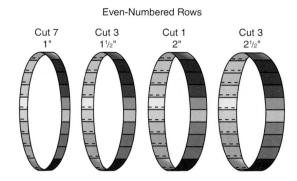

Even-Numbered Rows

Cut 7   Cut 3   Cut 1   Cut 3
1"   1½"   2"   2½"

Figure 5

Here's a Tip

Place a sticker on the focal print and label with the assigned row number. Referencing this fabric helps you develop the pattern before removing stitches between segments to create the rows.

3. Select the 1½" loop cut from tube 1. Remove the seam between one segment 1 and the adjacent segment 10 to make row 1 as shown in Figure 6. Mark the strip with the row number and place on a flat surface.

4. Referring to the Cutting/Pattern Diagram on page 27 for the design order and row numbers and widths, repeat step 3, removing the seam between segments on the odd and even loops to create the pattern shown. Mark each row with a number and place in numerical order on a flat surface to be sure that the design forms correctly. ***Note:*** *If you make a mistake, simply resew the seam to make the original loop and remove the correct seam.*

Row 1
1½"

Figure 6

5. When all rows are arranged and the pattern has formed correctly, start joining rows. Sew row 1 to row 2, matching seams as shown in Figure 7; press seam open. ***Note:*** *Seams should match easily because of the opposite pressing in the strip sets.*

Figure 7

6. Sew row 3 to row 4, row 5 to row 6, etc., placing the joined rows back in position after stitching to avoid disturbing the design. Continue joining in groups of two, then four, then eight, etc., until all rows are joined to complete the bargello center. Press all seams open to reduce bulk.

Completing the Top

1. Measure the bargello center through the horizontal and vertical centers. If sewing is perfect, it should measure 27" x 30½". ***Note:*** *If you have cut the border strips to the lengths given in the cutting list and they are not the same size as your center, trim the strips to fit your measurements or ease the strips onto the pieced top when sewing.*

2. Sew A strips to opposite long sides and B strips to the top and bottom of the bargello center; press.

3. Repeat step 2 with C and D strips to complete the piecing.

4. Arrange and fuse the prepared flower shapes on the upper right and lower left corners of the pieced top referring to Figure 8 for approximate distance from edge for flower placement.

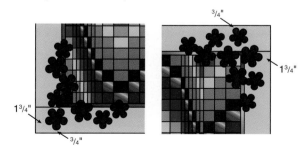

Figure 8

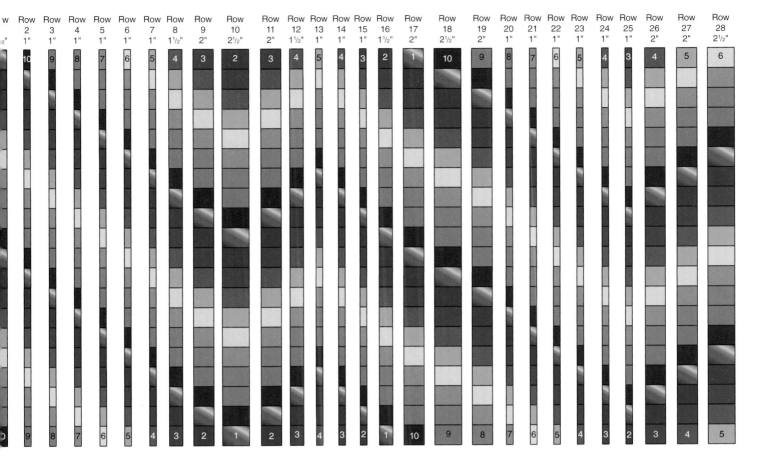

Olé

Cutting/Pattern Diagram

Refer to row widths and segment numbers when removing seams to form the pattern. All odd-numbered rows have seams pressed up and all even-numbered rows have seams pressed down.

5. Using thread to match the flower fabric and a machine straight stitch, stitch close to the edges of petals all around to secure as shown in Figure 9. *Note: Contrasting-color thread used in figure to make stitching show for illustration purposes only.*

Figure 9

Completing the Quilt

1. Sandwich the batting between the pieced top and a prepared backing piece; baste layers together. Quilt as desired.

2. When quilting is complete, remove basting and trim batting and backing fabric even with raw edges of the pieced top.

3. Prepare binding and stitch to quilt front edges, matching raw edges, mitering corners and overlapping ends. Fold binding to back side and stitch in place. ●

Inspiration

"I have always been fascinated by the beauty of bargello. It was the first class I taught and will always be a favorite of mine. The call for submissions brought back so many happy memories along with a challenge to hop out of my box just a little bit." —Carol Streif

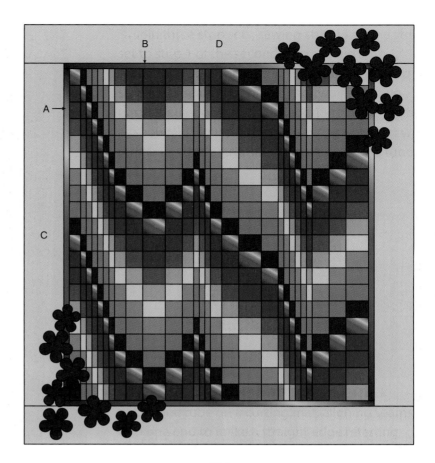

Olé
Placement Diagram 34$\frac{1}{2}$" x 38"

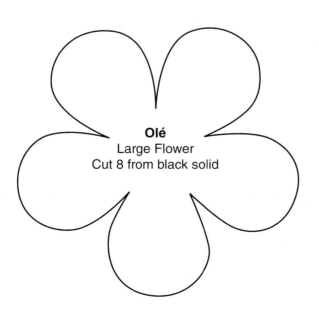

Olé
Large Flower
Cut 8 from black solid

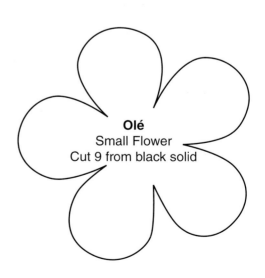

Olé
Small Flower
Cut 9 from black solid

Raw-Edge Fusible Appliqué

One of the easiest ways to appliqué is the raw-edge fusible-web method. Paper-backed fusible web motifs or individual pieces are fused to the wrong side of fabric, cut out and then fused to a foundation fabric and stitched in place by hand or machine.

Cutting Appliqué Pieces

1. Fusible appliqué motif pieces and individual pieces should be reversed for this technique.

2. Trace the appliqué shapes onto the paper side of paper-backed fusible web. Leave at least ¼" between shapes. Cut out shapes leaving a margin around traced lines. ***Note:*** *If doing several identical appliqués, trace reversed shapes onto template material to make reusable templates.*

3. Follow manufacturer's instructions and fuse shapes to wrong side of fabric as indicated on pattern for color and number to cut.

4. Cut out appliqué shapes on traced lines. Remove paper backing from shapes.

5. Again following fusible web manufacturer's instructions, arrange and fuse pieces to quilt referring to quilt pattern.

Stitching Appliqué Edges

Machine-stitch appliqué edges to secure the appliqués in place and help finish the raw edges with matching or invisible thread. Invisible thread can be used to stitch appliqués down when using the blanket or straight stitches. Do not use it for the satin stitch.

A short, narrow buttonhole or blanket stitch is most commonly used. Your machine manual may also refer to this as an appliqué stitch. Be sure to stitch next to the appliqué edge with the stitch catching the appliqué.

Practice turning inside and outside corners on scrap before stitching appliqué pieces. Learn how your machine stitches so that you can make the pivot points smooth.

1. To stitch outer corners, stitch to the edge of the corner and stop with needle in the fabric at the corner point. Pivot to the next side of the corner and continue to sew. You will often get a box on an outside corner.

2. To stitch inner corners, pivot at the inner point with needle in fabric. You will frequently see a Y shape in the corner.

3. You can also use a machine satin stitch or straight/running stitch. Turn corners in the same manner, stitching to the corners and pivoting with needle in down position.

4. Use a light- to medium-weight stabilizer behind an appliqué to keep the fabric from puckering during machine stitching.

5. To reduce the stiffness of a finished applique, cut out the center of the fusible web shape, leaving a ¼"-½" inside the pattern line. This gives a border of adhesive to fuse to the background and leaves the center soft and easy to quilt.

6. If an appliqué fabric is so light colored or thin that the background fabric shows through, fuse a lightweight interfacing to the wrong side of the fabric or fuse a piece of the appliqué fabric to a matching piece, wrong sides together, and then apply the fusible with a drawn pattern to one side.

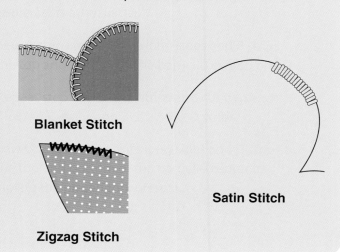

Blanket Stitch

Zigzag Stitch

Satin Stitch

Bargello-esque

Take the bargello technique one step further with this quilt that jumps outside the box using free piecing.

Design by Jenny Rekeweg
Quilted by Masterpiece Quilting

Skill Level
Intermediate

Finished Size
Quilt Size: 52" x 66"

Materials
Choose color groups to create the sections or blocks for the bargello medallion center of this quilt. The following choices reflect the choices for the sample quilt.

- Assorted 2" by fabric width strips from charcoal gray to nearly black solids, tonals or prints as darks to be mixed with colors
- 5 (2" by fabric width) strips assorted navy solids, tonals or prints in light to dark shades
- 5 (2" by fabric width) strips assorted yellow or gold solids, tonals or prints in light to dark shades
- 7 (2" by fabric width) strips assorted purple solids, tonals or prints in light to dark shades
- 8 (2" by fabric width) strips assorted green solids, tonals or prints in light to dark shades
- ⅝ yard black print
- 1 yard black solid
- 2½ yards total assorted black solids or tonals for outer borders
- Backing to size
- Batting to size
- Thread
- Basic sewing tools and supplies

Project Notes
Read all instructions before beginning this project.

Stitch right sides together using a ¼" seam allowance unless otherwise specified.

Refer to a favorite quilting guide for specific techniques.

Materials and cutting lists assume 40" of usable fabric width.

Fabric Notes

Challenge yourself to make the bargello section of this quilt completely from your stash. Join short fabric strips together on the short ends to make strips equal in fabric width.

Use strips in varying widths instead of all 2"-wide strips as specified in the Materials and Cutting lists.

There is no right or wrong placement of fabric. If you find that you need more of one color group, simply sew another color group to that strip and continue on. In this sample, strip sets were also made with gray and black.

Cutting

From black print:
- Cut 7 (2¼" by fabric width) binding strips.

From black solid:

- Cut 1 (8½" by fabric width) strip. Trim to make 1 (8½" x 33½") A strip.
- Cut 8 (1"–2½"-wide by fabric width) strips.

From black solids or tonals:

- Cut 3 (10" by fabric width) B strips.
- Cut 2 (25½" by fabric width) C strips.

Cutting Notes

There is no formula for making or cutting strip sets into segments. Be creative when cutting segments from the pieced strips.

Cut varying-width strips as well as some angled strips. Strips can be used in both horizontal and vertical placements and the order of strip use can be reversed.

If you need more strips from one color group, create a new strip set and cut segments.

Use solid strips to join segments as needed.

Make sections or blocks that finish at the sizes desired to fill the medallion. Alter your plan as needed and trim excess or add strips as you become more daring.

Designing the Bargello Center

1. Determine the finished size desired for the bargello medallion center (sample quilt center is approximately 33" x 33").

2. Create a rough sketch of finished bargello medallion center size dividing the area into sections or blocks. Figure 1 shows one way the 33"-square finished center could be put together. **Note:** *Use finished sizes in sketches but add ½" to these sizes for seam allowances when preparing blocks for construction.*

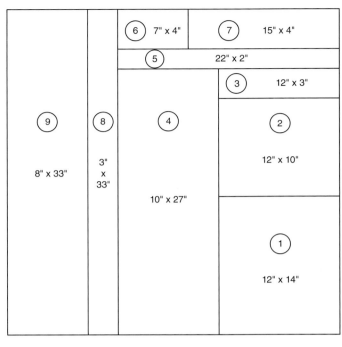

Figure 1

3. While creating a sketch adds a minimal amount of structure for planning the free piecing of the bargello sections or blocks, it is not necessary. To have even more design freedom, mark off the medallion area on a design wall or other flat surface. Add several strips to the medallion area where a section or block is desired, stitch them together, and then add more and stitch together again to make a section or block. Trim to size when section or block is approximately the desired size.

4. Remember that you are using the basics of bargello design to make each of the sections/blocks for the medallion. A bargello design is made up of strip sets that are then cut into different-width strips making strips of squares or rectangles of color. These strips are sewn together in staggered positions so that the colors wave throughout the area.

Completing the Bargello Center

Because of the nature of this technique, your quilt is unlikely to look exactly like the sample quilt, especially if you are using scraps and stash fabrics.

1. Select strips from a color group, gray-to-nearly black group, and one or two black solid strips.

2. Arrange strips as desired and join along the length to make a strip set; press seams in one direction.

3. Subcut the resulting strip set into a number of segments in varying widths from 1"–4", cutting two same-width segments of each size as shown in Figure 2 to make the strips needed for piecing.

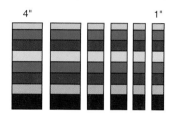

4"   1"

Figure 2

4. Join the strips on the ends as needed to make strips long enough to cut the longest measurement for the section you are working on.

5. Join the strips to make a section at least as large as the section you are working on (Figure 3).

Figure 3

6. Trim the stitched section to the size desired, adding ½" to the finished sizes when trimming as shown in Figure 4. Position the completed section or block within the medallion area.

Section 1

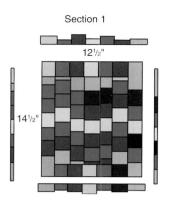

12½"

14½"

Figure 4

7. Repeat steps 1–6 with remaining strips to create bargello sections or blocks that will fill the medallion area of quilt; trim to size being sure to add ¼" seam allowance on all sides.

Completing the Quilt Top

1. Join the sections or blocks in groups to complete the bargello center referring to Figure 5. Press seams in each group before joining with another section or block.

Figure 5

2. Sew the A strip to the top of the pieced center; press seam toward A.

3. Join the B strips on the short ends to make a long strip; press. Subcut strip into two 10" x 41½" B strips. *Note: Sizes will vary with size of desired medallion. These measurements are for a 33" x 33" center.*

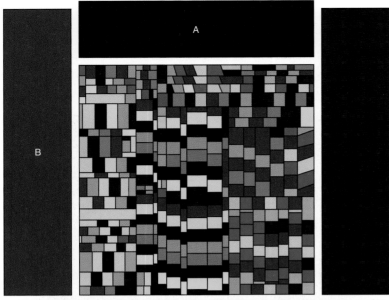

Bargello-esque
Assembly Diagram 52" x 66"

4. Sew the B strips to opposite sides of the pieced section; press seams toward B.

5. Join the C strips on the short ends to make a long strip; press. Subcut strip into one 25½" x 52½" strip.

6. Sew the C strip to the bottom of the pieced section to complete the quilt top; press seam toward C.

Completing the Quilt

1. Sandwich the batting between the pieced top and a prepared backing piece; baste layers together. Quilt as desired.

Inspiration

"My color scheme was inspired by Amish quilts. I strove to think outside the bargello box. I know that precise placement and exact cutting are not my favorite methods of quiltmaking, but I wanted the challenge of working with the bargello technique."
—*Jenny Rekeweg*

Bargello Notes

Bargello needlepoint embroidery originates from a series of chairs found in the Bargello palace in Florence. These flame-look stitch patterns have been adapted for quilting by using strip sets set up in the same type of color and geometric patterns.

The strip sets are cut in different widths and then offset vertically, or stepped, and stitched together.

Traditionally, this technique requires precise cutting and alignment to obtain the geometric patterns that reflect the needlepoint motifs.

Free piecing can be applied to almost any quilting technique if you understand the basics of that technique and are willing to let go of the rules.

When free piecing with bargello, strip sets are still cut in varying widths and stepped, but are often not stepped or positioned evenly, making the bargello areas look more erratic. And the sections or blocks are stitched together and trimmed to sizes to fill the medallion center.

To experiment with free-pieced bargello but still have a more traditional look, try drawing the medallion center out for specific-size sections or blocks. Follow traditional construction rules to make the individual sections or blocks of the medallion, but position them in more erratic ways within the medallion area by using sashing to set some on point or separate the horizontal and vertical sections or blocks from the square.

2. When quilting is complete, remove basting and trim batting and backing fabric even with raw edges of the pieced top.

3. Prepare binding and stitch to quilt front edges, matching raw edges, mitering corners and overlapping ends. Fold binding to back side and stitch in place. ●

Retro

The inspiration for this bargello quilt came from
a variation of a crocheted afghan.

Designed by Nancy Scott
Quilted by Masterpiece Quilting

Skill Level
Confident Beginner

Finished Size
Quilt Size: 60" x 78"

Materials
- ⅓ yard navy tonal
- ⅝ yard each dark teal tonal, and pink and green prints
- 1⅛ yards each red and aqua prints
- 1⅔ yards aqua tonal
- 1⅞ yards pink tonal
- 2⅔ yards yellow tonal
- Backing to size
- Batting to size
- Thread
- Basic sewing tools and supplies

Project Notes
Read all instructions before beginning this project.

Stitch right sides together using a ¼" seam allowance unless otherwise specified.

Refer to a favorite quilting guide for specific techniques.

Materials and cutting lists assume 40" of usable fabric width.

Cutting

From navy tonal:
- Cut 3 (2½" by fabric width) strips.

From dark teal tonal, & pink & green prints:
- Cut 6 (2½" by fabric width) strips each fabric.

From red & aqua prints:
- Cut 12 (2½" by fabric width) strips each fabric.

From aqua tonal:
- Cut 12 (2½" by fabric width) strips.
- Cut 8 (2¼" by fabric width) binding strips.

From pink tonal:
- Cut 21 (2½" by fabric width) strips.

From yellow tonal:
- Cut 33 (2½" by fabric width) strips.

Completing the Bargello Top
1. Arrange 2½"-wide strips in the order shown in Figure 1. Assign a number to each strip from 1–37.

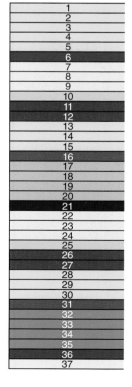

Figure 1

2. Join strips along length in numerical order, starting by sewing strip 1 to strip 2, strip 3 to strip 4, etc., and then joining the combined strips and so on until all 37 strips have been joined to make a strip set. Press seams open as you stitch.

3. Repeat steps 1 and 2 to make a total of three strip sets.

4. Sew strip 1 to strip 37 to make a tube as shown in Figure 2; press seam open. Repeat to make a total of three tubes.

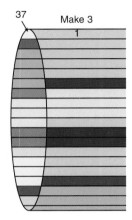

Figure 2

Here's a Tip

Lay the strips in numerical order on a flat surface. After joining two strips, place back in position to avoid disturbing the pattern.

5. Lay a tube on a cutting mat, aligning seams. Trim one end to make a straight edge. Repeat with remaining tubes.

6. Starting at the trimmed edge of each tube, subcut the tubes into 39 (2½") loops referring to Figure 3.

Cut 39
2½"

Figure 3

7. Remove a seam between segments in each loop to make a strip as indicated by the number in the left segment of each row as shown on the Cutting/Pattern Diagram on page 39. Count down 30 segments to the right and remove the seven remaining segments to make 60½"-long rows, again referring to the Cutting/Pattern Diagram. Set aside removed segments for another project.

8. Join the resulting strips in numerical order to complete the bargello section referring to the Assembly Diagram. *Note: Check that the fabrics in each strip are one position to the right or left of the same fabrics in the previous strip to make the pattern.*

9. When all strips are joined, press seams to one side to complete the top.

Completing the Quilt

1. Sandwich the batting between the pieced top and a prepared backing piece; baste layers together. Quilt as desired.

2. When quilting is complete, remove basting and trim batting and backing fabric even with raw edges of the pieced top.

3. Prepare binding and stitch to quilt front edges, matching raw edges, mitering corners and overlapping ends. Fold binding to back side and stitch in place. ●

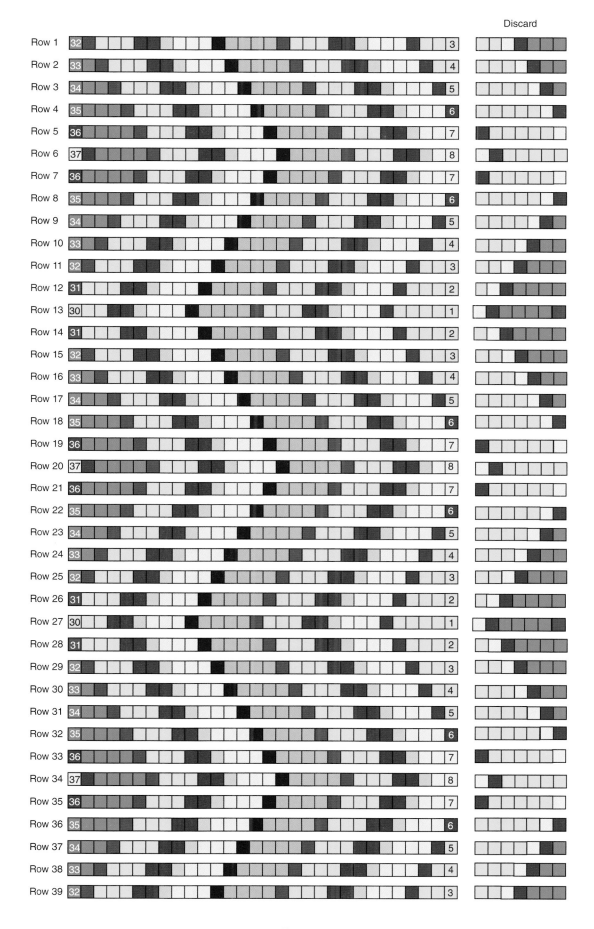

Row 1   32 ... 3
Row 2   33 ... 4
Row 3   34 ... 5
Row 4   35 ... 6
Row 5   36 ... 7
Row 6   37 ... 8
Row 7   36 ... 7
Row 8   35 ... 6
Row 9   34 ... 5
Row 10 33 ... 4
Row 11 32 ... 3
Row 12 31 ... 2
Row 13 30 ... 1
Row 14 31 ... 2
Row 15 32 ... 3
Row 16 33 ... 4
Row 17 34 ... 5
Row 18 35 ... 6
Row 19 36 ... 7
Row 20 37 ... 8
Row 21 36 ... 7
Row 22 35 ... 6
Row 23 34 ... 5
Row 24 33 ... 4
Row 25 32 ... 3
Row 26 31 ... 2
Row 27 30 ... 1
Row 28 31 ... 2
Row 29 32 ... 3
Row 30 33 ... 4
Row 31 34 ... 5
Row 32 35 ... 6
Row 33 36 ... 7
Row 34 37 ... 8
Row 35 36 ... 7
Row 36 35 ... 6
Row 37 34 ... 5
Row 38 33 ... 4
Row 39 32 ... 3

Retro
Cutting/Pattern Diagram
Refer to row and segment numbers when removing seams and
segments to form the pattern. There are 30 segments in each completed row.

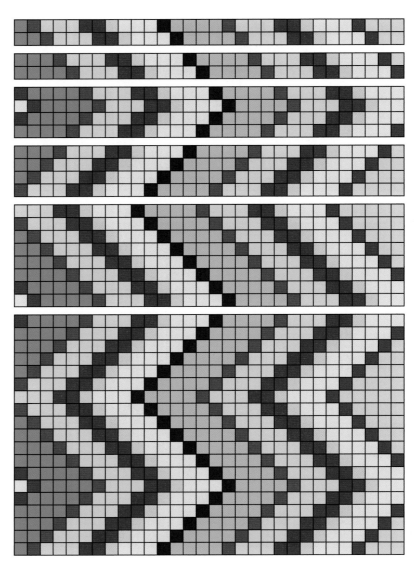

Retro
Assembly Diagram 60" x 78"

Peaks & Valleys

Placing progressive shades from light to dark grays and then black highlighted with red creates the peaks and valleys when using bargello piecing techniques.

Designed by Nancy Scott
Quilted by Masterpiece Quilting

Skill Level
Confident Beginner

Finished Size
Quilt Size: 54¼" x 73"

Materials
- ⅝ yard each of 11 different gray tonal fabrics: 1 each dark, medium and light charcoal, 2 medium gray, 2 medium/light gray and 4 light gray
- ⅞ yard red tonal
- 2 yards black solid
- Backing to size
- Batting to size
- Thread
- Basic sewing tools and supplies

Project Notes
Read all instructions before beginning this project.

Stitch right sides together using a ¼" seam allowance unless otherwise specified.

Refer to a favorite quilting guide for specific techniques.

Materials and cutting lists assume 40" of usable fabric width.

Cutting

From each gray tonal:
- Cut 6 (2½" by fabric width) strips (66 strips total).

From red tonal:
- Cut 6 (2½" by fabric width) strips.
- Cut 6 (1" by fabric width) A/B strips.

From black solid:
- Cut 6 (2½" by fabric width) strips.
- Cut 7 (3½" by fabric width) C/D strips.
- Cut 7 (2¼" by fabric width) binding strips.

Completing the Strip Sets
1. Select one 2½"-wide strip of each fabric. Arrange the 13 strips in the following order and assign a number for each strip: red 1, black 2, dark charcoal 3, medium charcoal 4, light charcoal 5, medium gray 6 and 7, medium/light gray 8 and 9, and light gray 10–13.

2. Sew strips together in pairs in numerical order, joining strip 1 to strip 2, strip 3 to strip 4, etc. Join the pairs and then groups of four and so on until you have joined all 13 strips in numerical order to create a strip set as shown in Figure 1. Press seams open. Repeat to make a total of six strip sets.

Make 6

Figure 1

3. Join three strip sets, sewing strip 13 of one strip set to strip 1 of the second strip set and strip 1 of the third strip set to strip 13 of the joined strip sets; press seams open. Join the two remaining unstitched edges of strips 1 and 13 to make a tube as shown in Figure 2; press seam open. Repeat with remaining three strip sets to make a second tube.

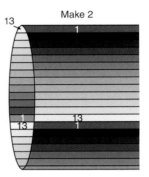

Figure 2

Completing the Bargello Center

1. Lay one tube on a cutting mat, aligning seams; trim one end to make a straight edge referring to Figure 3.

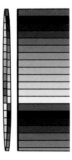

Figure 3

2. Starting at the trimmed end, cut the tube into loops of various widths as follows, using second tube when the first tube has been used: two 3½", three 1¾", six each 2" and 2¼", and nine 2½".

3. Select one 3½"-wide loop. Remove the seam between one red 1 segment and the adjacent light gray 13 segment to make strip 1 as shown in Figure 4. Label strip as strip 1 and place on a flat surface.

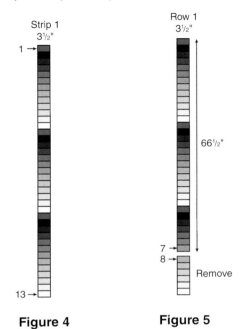

Figure 4   **Figure 5**

4. Count down 33 from the top red segment and open the seam between segments 7 and 8 as shown in Figure 5 to complete the 66½"-long row 1; place on a flat surface. Set aside the unused bottom portion for another project.

5. Select one 2½"-wide loop. Referring to Figure 6, remove the seam between one light gray 13 segment and the adjacent light gray 12 segment. Repeat step 4, counting down from the top light gray segment, and set aside the unused bottom portion. Label the longer portion of the strip as row 2 and place on a flat surface next to row 1.

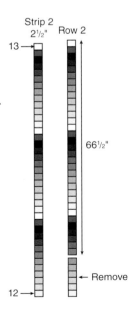

Figure 6

6. Continue the process as explained in steps 4 and 5 to make rows 3–26 referring to the Cutting/Pattern Diagram on page 46 for strip width and for removing seams and pieces to create the pattern.

7. When all rows are complete and arranged and the pattern has formed correctly, start joining rows. Sew row 1 to row 2, matching seams as shown in Figure 7; press seam open.

Figure 7

8. Sew row 3 to row 4, row 5 to row 6, etc., placing the joined rows back in position after stitching to avoid disturbing the design. Continue joining in groups of two, then four, then eight, etc., until all rows are joined to complete the bargello center. Press all seams open to reduce bulk.

Completing the Top

1. Measure the bargello center through the horizontal and vertical centers. If sewing is perfect, it should measure 47¾" x 66½".

2. Join the A/B strips on the short ends to make a long strip; press. Subcut strip into two each 1" x 66½" A strips and 1" x 48¾" B strips. *Note: Adjust lengths of strips as necessary to fit your quilt center's measurements taken in step 1.*

3. Sew A strips to opposite long sides and B strips to the top and bottom of the bargello center; press.

4. Repeat step 2 with C/D strips and cut two each 3½" x 67½" C strips and 3½" x 54¼" D strips.

5. Sew C strips to opposite long sides and D strips to the top and bottom of the bargello center to complete the pieced top; press.

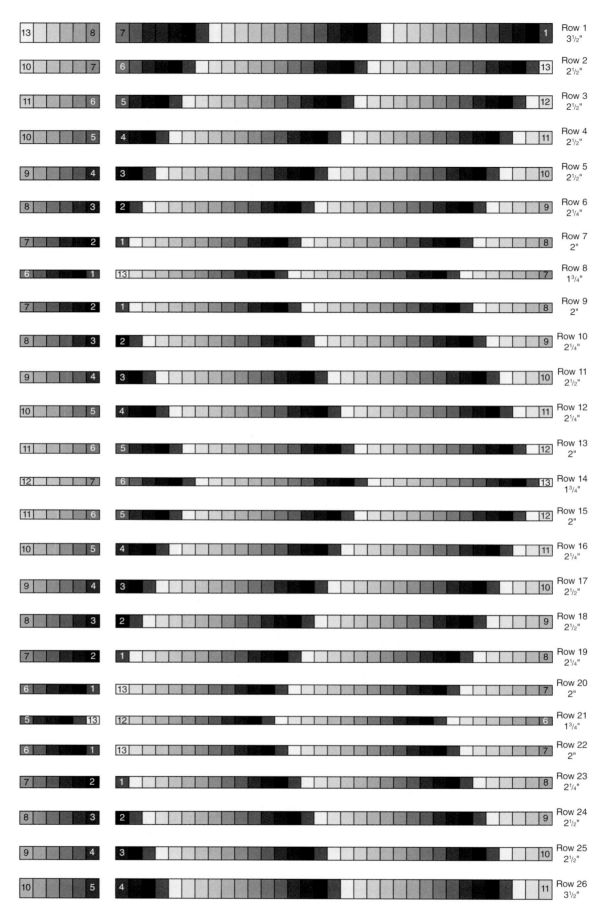

Peaks & Valleys
Cutting/Pattern Diagram
Refer to strip widths and segment numbers when removing seams and segments
to form the pattern. There are 33 segments in each completed vertical row.

Completing the Quilt

1. Sandwich the batting between the pieced top and a prepared backing piece; baste layers together. Quilt as desired.

2. When quilting is complete, remove basting and trim batting and backing fabric even with raw edges of the pieced top.

3. Prepare binding and stitch to quilt front edges, matching raw edges, mitering corners and overlapping ends. Fold binding to back side and stitch in place. ●

Inspiration

"I enjoy black-and-white photography, so this quilt reminds me of the gray scale found in black-and-white photos—with a pop of red, of course!" —Nancy Scott

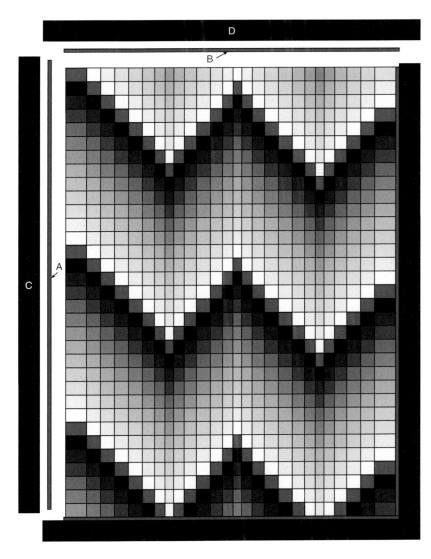

Peaks & Valleys
Assembly Diagram 54¼" x 73"

Special Thanks

Please join us in thanking the talented designers
whose work is featured in this collection.

Holly Daniels
And the Beat Goes On, page 8
Light-Headed Bargello, page 2

Gina Gempesaw
Robin's Egg Blue, page 12
Sunspots, page 18

Jenny Rekeweg
Bargello-esque, page 30

Nancy Scott
Peaks & Valleys, page 42
Retro, page 37

Carol Streif
Olé, page 23

Supplies

We would like to thank the following manufacturers who
provided materials to make sample projects for this book.

Light-Headed Bargello, page 2: Warm & White batting
from The Warm Company; Essential fabric collection
from Wilmington.

And the Beat Goes On, page 8: Soft & White batting from
The Warm Company; Cotton Couture solids from Michael
Miller Fabrics.

Robin's Egg Blue, page 12: Appliqué shapes from Sizzix;
American Spirit 70/30 batting from Fairfield.

Olé, page 23: Thermore® batting from Hobbs.

Bargello-esque, page 30: Digital quilting design from
TK Quilting & Design; Tuscany Collection wool batting
from Hobbs.

Retro, page 37: Digital quilting design from TK Quilting
& Design.

Peaks & Valleys, page 42: Digital quilting design from
TK Quilting & Design.

Bargello Quilts & Beyond is published by Annie's, 306 East Parr Road, Berne, IN 46711. Printed in USA. Copyright © 2015 Annie's.
All rights reserved. This publication may not be reproduced in part or in whole without written permission from the publisher.

RETAIL STORES: If you would like to carry this publication or any other Annie's publications, visit AnniesWSL.com.

Every effort has been made to ensure that the instructions in this publication are complete and accurate. We cannot, however, take responsibility for human error,
typographical mistakes or variations in individual work. Please visit AnniesCustomerService.com to check for pattern updates.

ISBN: 978-1-57367-955-8

1 2 3 4 5 6 7 8 9